SELL!

IDEA-RICH TECHNIQUES FOR SALES SUCCESS

Bob 'Idea Man' Hooey
Author of, Why Didn't I Think of That?

Nothing happens until someone sells something!

Foundational hint: Asking the right questions, the questions that **open conversations** with your prospective clients are a key to your long-term success as a top performing salesperson. They are also strategic in building and enhancing any business or organization. Know what they need and design something creative to better serve them. **This is where the sales magic happens.**

A word as we begin our journey together

"Sales can be a tough and sometimes complex, challenging, and confusing profession. It can also be fun!"

As a top performing professional salesperson, you need to identify individuals and organizations which you think may be interested in your product or service.

You approach people who may or may not want to talk to you. When the opportunity to meet with a prospective client arises, you need to convince them that your product or service is better and/or more cost effective than your competitors! You work diligently to build relationships. You may even close the sale! **That is just the beginning of the sales journey!**

Then, you work hard to keep your clients satisfied. You strive to earn their trust and secure their consideration of you for future or repeat sales. The rewards, both financial and professional, are tremendous.

As tough as the sales profession is, there are ways to improve your chances of long-term success. The overall sales process can be broken down into manageable and measurable steps.

Understanding each of these steps and following them can help you realize the maximum benefits from your sales efforts.

We are confident that, by the end of this *mini-sales success workbook*, you will have had the opportunity to access a substantial amount of information to help make you a better, more confident sales professional who knows how to **'Create Repeat Buyers'**. Notice we call it a workbook because we challenge you to do the homework. ☺

Table of Contents

Sales is a essentially a systematic process of being open to leads, working to move them into serious prospects and finally, converting them to long-term clients and customers.

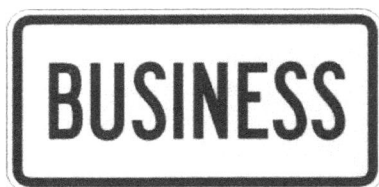

BUSINESS

8 Field-Proven Tips to Increase Your Income

Most of us in business (selling profession) are driven by goals. One goal is to find ways to increase our sales (income) and reduce our time demands in doing so. **Is this an achievable goal?** YES! One of the ways of doing that is in converting your 'one time' customers into regular buyers/clients who come back again and again to buy from you. Better yet, they bring their friends, too. This is the best way of increasing your income.

Finding ways to get your potential and current customers to 'buy in larger quantities' is a valuable goal. Of course, finding new customers and getting qualified leads and referrals from existing customers is still a valid goal. **Here are some practical tips**, which, when applied, allow you to hone your sales skills and accomplish all of these goals.

Become an Avid Reader (Leaders are readers!)

There are essentially only two ways to learn new things. One is through your own experience; the other, more effective way, is 'leveraged learning' through other people's experiences. Professionals are readers in search of new ideas, methods, and training materials to equip themselves to better prospect, qualify, sell, and then successfully build long-term customer relationships. What profitable ideas have you learned from someone else lately? **Buying this book** was a great start. 😊

Have Fun Selling and Serving!

You spend more time working than any other activity in your life, so why not enjoy the time you invest in the selling /customer service process? Don't just think of selling as work. View it as enjoyable as any of your favorite family, leisure, or sports activities. When you get good at it – that's what happens anyway. People 'earn and learn' more in times of enjoyment!

Attend Training Seminars to Hone Your Selling Skills

Don't wait on your company to lead or train you! Invest in yourself and your selling future. There is no better way to learn a skill than attending a seminar or selling boot camp by street smart, successful sales experts. This is a true success secret from the business and selling superstars!

Delegate Effectively

Most of your selling/customer service time should be spent meeting with prospects and customers – not just doing administrative busy work! Follow-up and paperwork are a solid part of the selling/customer service process, but don't allow yourself to get bogged down in this area.

Subscribe to Informative Newsletters (read and apply)

Subscribe to successful 'selling' and motivational newsletters to keep up to date on hot new techniques and ideas for your business. There's nothing better than getting a regular helping of fresh hot new ideas and perspectives from experts on business or selling. Invest time to read, reflect, and ACT!

Have the Right Attitude about Selling, Service, and Business

The right attitude about selling, service, and business will carry you through, regardless of what challenges or obstacles are thrown in your way. Learning to view prospecting as natural and selling as an ongoing event will make you a champion. It will also make you wealthy! Building solid relationships which generate repeat business begins with the right attitudes.

Don't Make Excuses for Your Lack of (Selling) Success

Under-performers love to have a scapegoat to blame for their failures or lack of achievement.
If you talk to them, it is always something – the economy, the competition, the product, or the price… anything other than

'themselves' and their lack of commitment or performance. As a successful businessperson, you realize that your success, or lack of it, is totally, 100% your responsibility! Take personal leadership of your (selling/service) role and take corrective steps to add to your skills and succeed.

Welcome Your Mistakes as Learning Opportunities

Everyone makes mistakes. Successful professionals realize mistakes are a part of their learning curve and maximize the lesson from each one. ***"Next time I will do _____ "*** is their professional response to a new learning experience. Don't spend your time worrying or feeling victimized by mistakes. Instead spend 99% of your time thinking about a solution, as do the selling/service superstars! It works!

A note from Bob: My wife gave me a couple of coffee mugs for our place in the country last Christmas. As I drank from one of them this morning, I paused for a moment to consider its words of wisdom.

**"Behind every success is effort...
behind every effort is passion...
behind every passion is someone with the courage to try."
And on the inside lip: "GO For It!"**

In the exciting game of sales this is certainly true. Often it is taking that next step, to make one more call, one more follow-up or sales letter, that makes the difference. It is taking one more step in the direction of your dreams to capture and create the future you desire. It is taking one more *decisive* step that allows you to pull away from the pack and win and keep the business.

So, what is your next step?

Mistakes made by NEW, lazy, or ineffective sales staff

- Why is it that some senior or seasoned sales staff are often more effective and productive in their sales efforts?
- Why are some sales staff better at building long-term, profitable relationships that result in repeat sales and multiple referrals?

Could it be that they've learned these simple points that help them sell better and to build more profitable client relationships?

As previously discussed, companies and selling professionals that take good care of their clients generally retain them for an extended period.

For ineffective sales staff or newer sales personnel that lack the proper training, there are **some pitfalls** here as well.

Lack of preparation. Someone once said that *"Success happens when opportunity meets preparedness."* Your level of preparedness directly impacts your credibility with a client and can make or break the establishment of a trust relationship. This means knowing your product or service as well as your firm's policies and procedures. It also means having a good understanding of what your competition provides in these same areas. Prepare yourself to win and work to make sure you become a trusted advisor in your client dealings.

Why is it we feel we can simply go through our life and our careers winging it or going with the flow? Why is it so few invest the time to prepare themselves to win, to grow, and to succeed?

Not listening. 90% of salespeople never listen or listen ineffectively and are subsequently doomed to frustration and lack of success in their selling activities. Active listening is the key foundation to discovering your client's current and future needs and to determining your ability to meet them. **Asking questions and listening carefully** through the interview or qualification part of the conversation is where you build solid foundations for later sales success.

I remember being interviewed by a national Canadian magazine on sales and being asked many questions about closing, overcoming objections, and such. I told the interviewer that, "…most of the situations they presented (examples mentioned by the interviewer) could be dealt with by more effective qualifying. **Ask questions earlier in the sales conversation and listen to what your clients tell you.** Their answers will provide the guidance you need to help them (customers) make effective buying decisions."

Failing to ask for the order. This is the most critical part of your sales conversation. Yet, most of the studies I've read show that 70% of all salespeople never ask for the order. A larger percentage *never* ask for additional orders. Do you?

I remember asking a group of home furnishing salespeople in Wisconsin, *"Would you like to learn how to double or even triple your sales income in the next year?"* Hands went up across the auditorium. I paused for dramatic effect and told them the secret, *"Simply ask for the order at least twice in the sales conversation."* I went on to say, *"Most of you are not asking even once!"* They were visibly shocked. One of their leading saleswomen told me afterwards that I was right on the money.

Poor or no follow up. Follow up and follow through is where 90% of all great sales are made. Conversely, this is where most sales staff miss the opportunity to gain and maintain a client. This is where the real sale begins (post purchase) and the relationship is built for long-term profitability. I am continually surprised at how few salespeople follow up on leads or even keep in touch with current clients. The simple act of keeping in touch could provide the leverage to a long and mutually beneficial relationship.

Small Thinking. Want bigger sales? You must think bigger. Ask these questions: "How high is too high? What is my maximum potential? What is the lifetime value of my relationship with this client? What is the potential for referrals from this client?"

Think big and act accordingly to see your sales results soar. Dream it and then move confidently ahead to create foundations under your dreams.

Failing to establish and/or maintain rapport. This can be a killer if you have any aspirations of maintaining a mutually profitable relationship over a long period with your clients.

Investing time, at the beginning of your sales conversation, is crucial to your success. Building on that rapport by keeping in touch can separate you from the lackluster salespeople in your field. It will also help attract clients who will become active cheerleaders and champions on your behalf.

Failing to commit and establish oneself as an expert in your field. People like to deal with (and talk about) people who know what they are doing. Failing to present yourself as such negatively impacts or restricts your future earnings with clients.

Do your homework so you know your products, services, and your industry. People love to work with people who know what they are doing and who earn their trust by their demonstrated expertise and credibility. A bit of study now can make a major difference in your future earnings and success.

Ask yourself how you fare in each of these above areas:
- Would you give yourself a passing mark?
- Which areas need a little work?
- How will you change what you do to make sure you give your clients the most professional service possible?

Give your sales team a chance to win by reminding them of these success tactics. Remind them to keep focused and keep working toward their goals of helping the client make a decision that is both good for the client and profitable over the long haul for the company.

How can you change and/or help your sales team make the changes necessary to become a professional salesperson/team and provide continued value-added service?

Getting your clients to sell you

Here are a few idea-rich tips to help engage your clients in recommending and selling you to their friends and contacts.

Go the extra mile!

One of the most effective activities in building loyalty and turning clients into repeat buyers, raving fans, and champions of your service or business is to go the extra mile. By this we mean doing more than normal to help them achieve the success or satisfaction they really wanted.

- Have you ever experienced having someone going way beyond what would normally be included in your purchase?
- Did it catch your attention and make you take notice?
- How can you do this with your clients?

"Outstanding people have one thing in common: An absolute sense of mission." Zig Ziglar

Understanding why people buy... and re-position yourself to take advantage of that reasoning

People make purchases, accept offers, or decide to frequent a specific store or vendor for a variety of reasons. They buy into benefits. The better you understand the reasons they buy, as related to your product or service, the better you will be equipped to convince them to buy from you. Your research and conversations with them can uncover the keys to gaining and retaining them as customers. *'Idea-rich customer service'* is offering me what I really need, not just what you sell or what I ask for!

The following benefits reflect the reasons people buy in order of importance. Remember each prospect is different, as is each product or service. Your product or service might not offer all these benefits. That might be ok, or maybe not – you decide! However, is there some way to modify or position your product or service to offer each benefit?

Unleash your Business Potential - offer customers more reasons to deal with you! Here are ten reasons why people make decisions to buy or engage in the services of a professional or business.

1. To make money/acquire or possess something
Describe how your product or service offers me the potential for profit or a potential gain.

2. To save money or prevent future loss
Describe how your product/service offers ways to save me money.

3. To save time
Describe how your product/service can save me time.

4. For recognition
Describe how your product/service offers me recognition or perceived status.

5. For security/peace of mind
Describe how your product/service offers me security or peace of mind.

6. For convenience/comfort
In what ways does your product/service provide for my convenience or comfort?

7. For flexibility
How is your product/service rate in flexibility? In what areas? How?

8. For satisfaction/reliability/pleasure or entertainment
How does your product/service stack up in these areas? Why is that important to me?

9. For status or pride of ownership/ gratify ego or impress others
How does your product/service add to my status or pride of ownership?

10. For health reasons
Is there some way that your product/service will contribute to my health?

Drop me an email and I'll send you the full list of **50 emotional reasons why people buy**. bob@ideaman.net

Understanding the answers to these questions will give you an edge in gaining, serving, and keeping your customers. Being able to present your product or service from this perspective in meeting your client's needs, by appealing to their desired benefits, can be critical to your success.

The more you know about your client, your product/service, and your competition, the better equipped you are to effectively do business. Can you think of any other reasons why people would want to do business with you?

Advancing your sales techniques
Idea-rich strategies to attract repeat buyers

Being and remaining successful in the sales game means making the best use of your time and increasing the overall volume of profitable sales you bring into your company. Successful, top-level sales professionals know this and 'deliberately' focus their energies on the most important aspects of the selling process – acquiring, serving, and keeping their clients.

For most businesses, the costs associated with acquiring a new client are about 5 to 10 times greater than securing an order from an existing client. Yet most companies and many ineffective salespeople neglect the more profitable, long-term relationships with their current clientele; choosing instead to focus their energy on prospecting – attempting to close new clients.

- **New clients provide growth.**
- **Mining existing clients provides profit and sustained, long-term growth.**

In this mini sales success workbook (*we chose workbook for a reason – it is meant for you to work though, not just read*) we will investigate 'why' and 'how' you should act if creating repeat buyers is your sales success goal. We outlined tools and techniques which have been field-proven by North America's top performing sales professionals. Tools you can apply – and profit from – tomorrow when you return to your sales environment.

In business, there are three main approaches to increasing your business and gaining increased sales results:

1. **Increase the number** of clients;
2. **Increase the average size of the sale** per client;
3. **Increase the frequency** at which a client returns to buy again.

There are many great sales books on the market. My friend **Brian Tracy** has written many of them, including '*The Art of Closing the Sale.*' **SELL!** focuses primarily on tools and techniques which target the second approach. It will help you more effectively pre-qualify your prospects by evaluating their lifetime value as a client. Marketing (focusing on increasing the number of clients) is also important and we'll share a few ideas on that as we work through this publication.

Not surprisingly, focusing on the second approach, with an emphasis on ensuring that your current clients receive exceptional client satisfaction, will subsequently generate new clients. **People love to share** a good experience and will start selling or referring you to their friends and business associates. **Success tends to expand and spread**!

This is the best used secret we've observed in top performers and their organizations. It will help you to develop a simple account management system focused on increased sales and overall account growth. Once this account management system is in place, you will be able to direct your energies to the clients who will profitably grow with you; and, by so doing, realize your maximum potential as a committed selling professional.

According to a Boston based consulting firm, the average Fortune 500 Company could instantly double its revenue growth rate with a 5% increase in client retention, and a small to mid-size company could double its profits in ten years by simply increasing its client retention rate by 5%. Research results draw an interesting parallel in process, timeline, and results for profitability in small, mid-size, and larger firms. People buy for various reasons and buying often has an emotional attachment. Knowing and understanding the emotions behind the various reasons why people buy will allow you to position or re-position yourself and your company to provide additional products and services over an extended period. **Applied knowledge delivers real selling power.**

A few thoughts on setting sales success goals, 'even' in tough times

Ultimately, the *measurement and review of your value* to your firm, as a salesperson, is directly tied to your ability to sell.

Your leadership team will look at your sales volume at a specific time during your firm's term of measurement. That look might be monthly, quarterly, a bi-yearly performance appraisal, or year end. But it will happen and it makes good sense to be both aware of it and prepare to ensure your sales results *stand up* under scrutiny.

You may be providing intrinsic value to your team and your firm through your activities. However, when all is said and done, your sales results are the primary factor used to evaluate your performance and promotion. That is the harsh truth.

Sales master W. Clement Stone challenged his sales team to ***"Set a goal so BIG, that if you achieved it, it would blow your mind."***

This is not a time to play it safe, nor is it time to listen to those (even those who may be relatively successful in selling) who would tell you setting goals is a waste of time. It isn't a waste of your time. Your success and growth in the sales field will be directly tied to your ability to formally set and achieve your goals.

Set a realistic goal that will push you; one that will stretch you in its achievement. Set a goal worthy of your potential and then work diligently to achieve it. **Prepare yourself to win!**

In sales, life, and business we have proven results and thousands of stories of people who formally set goals who went on to substantially greater success than their counterparts. You can too if you *'plan and then work your plan.'* This investment of your time in setting your goals for the year, and revisiting and revising them as needed, provides the roadmap for your sales success; *'more so'* in tough times when every sale counts.

Take a few minutes and go through a brief planning process considering your **BIG Goal**. Depending on your focus (sales, commission, units) here is how you might do it.

1. Set your income or sales target (choose which works best for you) or,
2. Set your commission and/or bonus target (if this works better for you) or,
3. Divide your yearly target (#1) by the average commission and/or bonus per sale (#2). If you need help, go back over your previous year, or talk to your sales manager. This calculation should yield an annual 'unit' sales target needed to reach your sales target, income, or commission.
4. You can then divide this number (either #1, #2, #3) by 12 to give your monthly target, or divide it by 50 (average number of weeks with 2 weeks of holidays) to get your weekly number.

See it! Write it! Achieve it!

However, you work it out, it is a good idea to break your 'BIG' sales goal into measurable weekly and/or monthly results. That makes it easier to track your success and make changes if you notice you need to bump it up to keep on track. My friend, **Marc LeBlanc** suggests making every month a symbolic New Year.

Now what? What is next if you are serious about meeting this BIG goal?

*   What activities (average) do you need to be involved in on a weekly or monthly basis to reach your calculated results?
*   How many outbound sales calls do you need to make to explore or set up an initial sales interview?

- How many (average) sales interviews or demonstrations (daily, weekly, monthly, quarterly) do you need to qualify a customer where an order can be placed, or a proposal created?
- How many (average) proposals or contracts need to be delivered daily (weekly, monthly, and quarterly) to close the deal?

If needed, you can go back over your last year's results (keep in mind you are setting a big goal that will stretch you) to get a sense of what is needed to get to the sale. When you have worked out your sales numbers in relation to your BIG sales goal, then you are ready. Being prepared is one of the secrets to being successful in sales.

Henry Ford said, "Before everything else, being ready is the Secret of Success!"

YES ☑
NO ☐

Keep these numbers close to you as a reference guide to chart your progress. Measure them frequently and honestly and decide where you need help. Ask for help when you need it.

- Do you need help in prospecting or qualifying?
- Do you need help demonstrating your firm's products or explaining your firm's services, policies, etc.?
- Do you need help in closing?
- Do you need help in follow up to create additional sales and repeat business?

"High expectations are the key to everything."
Sam Walton

What's YOUR U.S.P.?

It might be valuable for you to sit down with your team or staff and think about what your Unique Selling/Service Proposition really is. What advantage do you have or need to separate yourself from your competitors both locally and globally?

Seriously consider each of these typical USPs. Some might be applicable; many will simply be an 'ME too' response. It's not unique if everyone does it or can offer it. Be willing to dig deep and prove your points here.

- Selection
- Big or volume discounts
- Advice or assistance
- Top of the line (high end)
- Speedy service
- Service beyond the basics
- Convenience
- Better warranty/guarantee (compared to whom?)

What is your GAP?

If you are like me: Perhaps there is a **GAP** between what you say and what you do? Perhaps there is a **GAP** between what you believe and what is true? Perhaps there is a **GAP** between your dreams and your reality? Perhaps there is a **GAP** between your intentions and your actions? Perhaps there is a **GAP** between you and your clients?

That is, for the most part, a normal situation in each of our lives. Each of us needs to work on reducing the **GAPS** in our lives or in filling them if we are truly committed to growing and becoming more productive in our lives and careers. As professional salespeople we hone our skills to reduce the **GAPS, or at least build bridges for our clients.**

Building a successful sales career or business

To be effective in sales and business in general, we must deal with these three critical areas as they directly relate to our clients and their ever-changing needs:

- **Pain**
- **Gain**
- **Sustain**

Your profitability and long-term viability will be impacted to the degree that you work with your clients to affect these diverse areas or concerns. Each area has its focus and resulting profit center.

If we help people with their **pain** - will they need us when it is gone? This is a good starting point for client engagement. Dealing with their pain should be a solid part of your business, but I would hope you would be able to go a bit further with them.

Helping them **gain** offers a bit more opportunity to serve and build longer-term mutually beneficial relationships. Clients love us when we help them make gains in their business. **But there is still more!**

If you can work with them through their pain, help them gain in the process, and then take them through by helping them grow and **sustain** growth, you will be a major part of their team for years to come.

Repeat buyers are created by building on this three-fold premise. Clients will deal with you time and time again if you help them see and receive the value you provide.

- How do you currently sell in relation to these three areas?

- Are there areas where you know you can make changes in your approach to be more effective in working with your clients for the long haul?

As mentioned earlier, when all is said and done, there are essentially three productive ways to increase your sales or business:

- **Increase the number of clients** you attract and retain to deal with you and your company',
- **Increase the average size of the sale** for each client,
- **Increase the frequency** or number of times each client returns and buys.

Look for ways to attract more clients in the services and product mix you offer. How many reasons can you give them as an incentive or reason to choose you?

Condition your mind to seek creative solutions and/or breakthrough ideas. Investigate other industries. Look at their success stories and best practices and see if they hold a secret that you can creatively transfer to your business.

Fed-Ex simply adapted the central distribution system used by the banking system for his courier delivery. Fed-Ex founder, **Fred Smith**, did well with this transplanted breakthrough!

Often the secret to your success and in your differentiation from your competitors lies in the operations and activities of businesses in a different industry. What can you learn and transfer to yours? Hmmm

As fellow author **Jay Abraham** says: **"Breakthroughs let you outthink, out leverage, out market, out sell, out impact, out defend, out maneuver, and continuously outwit your competition at every level."**

Look for breakthrough or transferable ideas in marketing, innovation, operations, sourcing, technology, systems, process, selling, financing, product mix, service list, and distribution. Every area of your business exists to support what you are doing for your clients. Look for methods or tweaks to make each area serve you and your client.

"To build a long-term, successful enterprise, when you don't close a sale, open a relationship." **Patricia Fripp**

How about looking for ways to add-on or cross-sell? This is one of the success secrets of the more effective and profitable selling professionals who maximize every client contact.

Adding-on helps you move the client to a larger or superior product, package, or service. It is based on having a thorough understanding of the client's intended use and recognizing that the basic product or service may fail to meet the real needs of your client. Remember, **you are committed to their best interests.** You are doing your client a disservice if you allow them to buy something that will 'not' meet their needs. Not to mention that when doing so, you are building in a possible unsatisfied result, which will impact your repeat sales potential.

Cross-selling introduces your client to additional products or service. Offer them alternatives that perform better and are in their best interest. Phone service providers like Telus, Fido, and Bell do this well with bundling: Voice mail, call waiting, auto call back, 2nd line, autodial, calling cards, caller ID, 3rd line for security, and 4th line for fax, cable and computer information delivery systems. So, do Bell, Shaw and other media or telecommunication providers.

Test market your product mix and services offered. This single secret from exceptional marketers works at every level in business and sales. Check your marketing or sales messages and tweak them to be more effective.

Experiment with your Website(s), advertising, promotional materials, sales and direct mail letters, live sales presentations and in store demos, guarantees, USP's, pricing points, volume purchase options and discounts, or financing. See what works!

Nothing is sacred. Keep refining what you've got until you find something that is effective. Then, continue to update your services and/or products to keep them fresh and relevant to the changing marketplace and evolving needs of your clients.

Look for ways to **form strategic alliances** or co-op with those companies or non-competitive sales reps who are already dealing with the people you would like to attract. Selectively network or collaborate with companies or reps who have already earned your prospective clients' trust and respect.

If you offer complimentary, non-competitive services or products that assist others in better serving their clients, you will find a more favorable response. This can create double wins for you, those with whom your joint venture, and your respective clients who are better served.

You'll frequently see **Starbucks** coffee shops in **Chapters** bookstores across Canada, as well as in many **Canada Safeway** stores. This provides a double win for both companies.

You frequently see bank machines and, in some cases, mini branches in grocery stores for the same reasons. I've seen **Kinko's** set up in larger hotel complexes and convention centers in the US.

Look for opportunities to offer this kind of connection to people who want to deal with your clients and who offer something you either don't offer or are unable to do so profitably now.

Professional example: Years ago, I came up with an idea for groups of speakers to co-operatively promote and market their services on a regional basis. We each contributed to the creation and maintenance of a website and did some print advertising to self-promote during the year.

Please visit **www.AlbertaSpeakers.com** to see what we have done. We are in our 11th year of working together and most of the speakers on the site have been there since we launched. Who would you like to have as a strategic alliance?

Homework: Yes, we are giving you a homework assignment.

Explore and discuss your ideas on how to apply these principles in your sales process and in how you interact with your current customers and potential clients.

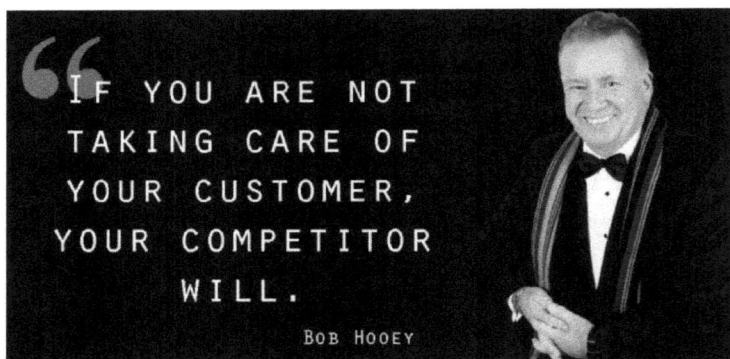

> IF YOU ARE NOT TAKING CARE OF YOUR CUSTOMER, YOUR COMPETITOR WILL.
>
> BOB HOOEY

This quote has taken wings and is showing up around the world, even on a training room wall in Johannesburg, South Africa. It has been featured in INC, Fast Company, and many other top business magazines. Guess it strikes a chord! Are you taking care of your customer? This is the secret of long-term sales success my friends.

Five successful techniques for generating increased sales

The funny thing, as top performing professionals we need to consistently improve on our sales success. **There is no static in selling!** We need to be working on gaining new customers, repeat business, and, of course, referrals just to keep current; let alone move up to the next level. Let's explore five field-proven success techniques you can use to generate an increase in your sales. You'll find them simple to use and effective for building any business.

Adding Something 'New' or improved to 'The Mix'

Every time you add something 'new' to your business, product, or service mix you create another new opportunity to get more sales. Each time you make a tweak or improvement you **open a door for new client conversations**. For example, something as simple as adding new information on your website creates another selling opportunity when prospects and customers visit your site to access or view the new information. When was the last time you updated your web pages and, at least, changed the dates?

Adding a new product or service to the list of those you already offer can produce a big increase in sales. Even refreshing in-store displays help create this effect. The added service or product can increase your sales opportunities in three different ways:

- It attracts 'new' customers who were not 'initially' interested in your current products and services.
- It generates repeat sales from 'existing' customers who also want to have your new product or services.
- It enables you to get 'bigger' sales by combining 2 or more items into special package or bundle offers.

Become a Value-added Resource to Your Customers

Look for ways you can be a trusted resource for your prospects and customers. Supply them with relevant, free information on how to do something more effectively, enhance their business, or save money. Refer them to allied professionals who can help them in areas you don't cover or provide.

You get another opportunity to sell something every time they come back to you for help. This enhances your credibility and builds a trust relationship. *For example, with our Secret Selling Tips we added a weekly Motivational Sales Quotes service.*

Separate (differentiate) Yourself from Your Competition

Find or create a reason for customers to do business with you instead of with someone else offering the same or similar products or services. What makes you 'unique'? For example, do you provide faster results, easier procedures, personal attention, or a better guarantee?

Determine the unique sales/service proposition (USP) or competitive advantage you offer to clients/customers that your competitors do not offer. Promote that advantage/benefit in all your advertising. Give your prospects valid reasons to do business with you instead of with your competition and you'll automatically get more sales.

Focus and Promote the 'End-result' or net benefit

Your customers don't really want your product or service. They want the benefit enjoyed by using it. They don't really care about your background, your services, or even your products. What they 'really' care about is the 'results' they get from using you instead of someone else.

For example, car buyers want convenient transportation with a certain image. Business opportunity seekers want personal and financial freedom for themselves and their family. Sales Managers want successful programs that will equip and motivate their sales teams to be more profitable in the selling game.

Make sure your web pages, sales letters, other sales materials, or media are promoting the end-result or true benefits your customers really want and need.

Anticipate and Prepare for Change

Change is the biggest challenge to your sales or business success. The days are history when a business could constantly grow by simply repeating what it did successfully in the past, or even recently. Aggressive, innovative, global competitors and rapidly changing technology make staying with the status quo impossible if you want to survive and remain profitable.

Think about some larger well-known firms that are in trouble or have gone out of business in recent years. In most cases, their 'failure' was primarily due to ignoring changes in technology, customer needs, competition, and changes in the market or other factors that might have been incorporated into their working environment. If they'd been awake and willing to change, they might still be profitable. Now they are dead or near dead!

Expect change and actively prepare for it. Don't wait until your income declines to act. Develop the habit of looking for early warning signs that something is changing. Then aggressively confront it before you start to lose customers.

Hint: Insure yourself against the impact of change by increasing the number of complementary products and services you offer and by using a variety of different marketing methods. Only a small portion of your total business will be affected if the sales of one product fall or the response to one marketing method declines. Always adjust what you do to be more effective in finding and keeping your customers.

- How many of these field-proven techniques have you overlooked or ignored?
- How many of these are currently being used in your selling or business strategies?
- When will you act on some new ones?

Follow-up is essential if you want to succeed in business

If you want to build long-term repeat buyers and referrals, this should be your first focus with your client relationships. If you want to be successful, build a system to follow-up with all your (clients) customers. The average business only hears from 4% of their dissatisfied customers. According to **Lee Resources**, 91% of unhappy customers will not 'willingly' do business with you again. However, resolve their concerns in their favor and 70% will give you another chance and deal with you again.

This is where surveys and callbacks are essential. If you wait for them to let you know of a 'problem', you will lose their business forever. Check to see what people are saying about you on-line (e.g. Twitter, LinkedIn, Facebook, Yelp, Instagram, etc.).

This **'unfiltered' customer feedback** on their sales experience can be invaluable to the smart business professional. If you are aware of a problem, you have the chance to do something about it and prove you really want to serve them.

The fun part: when you fix their concern, many of them move into being raving fans and champions for you.

Tell descriptive, idea-rich stories that engage our minds, create value, and help sell on many levels

Customer service and sales is not 'just' having products or services to sell your clients. It is as much about 'how' you help them experience or investigate potential purchases. It is about being dedicated to helping them make intelligent, value-added decisions that make their life or business better.

Perhaps you've heard or been taught that sharing **Features, Advantages** and **Benefits** is a more effective approach to create 'value' than just feature dumping on our prospective customers or teams. It is! But do we effectively do that in our sales, service, and leadership conversations?

Let me share a simple experience where a young shoe salesman did this very well.

We all need shoes and hopefully, since we are on our feet a lot, we select some that are comfortable, yet stylish to wear when we are at work. At least that is my story.☺

Years ago, I was doing some sailing in Puerto Vallarta, Mexico. One afternoon I was enjoying a quiet break while window shopping. Along the way, a very stylish, yet simple, pair of two-tone loafers caught my eye in a little shoe store off the quaint cobblestone street. Thinking I was 'only looking'; I stepped into the store to check them out. I picked them up and quickly put them down, as my initial reaction was, *"Wow... they are not cheap!"*

My young and *very wise* shoe expert approached and engaged me in conversation about my visit to his store, to Puerto Vallarta, and what I did for a living. I made the mistake of telling him I was a professional speaker, leadership success coach, and business success trainer who traveled sharing ideas on how others could be more successful in their lives, leadership careers, sales, etc. (Guess he figured I could afford them... smile.)

Picking up the shoes and holding them with reverent care, he said, "You know, when you wear these traditional loafers, you're going to have a big smile on your face because 'one of the great things' about these shoes is they're soft calfskin leather with a full leather lining. And, as you wear them, they will mold to the shape of your feet, giving you a 'custom-made' feel."

He continued, "It would be fun to walk around in custom-made shoes, don't you think?"

He could have just said, "These shoes are all leather, which is flexible, making them very comfortable." On the surface that sounds good, doesn't it?

However, what he said 'engaged' me and was more effective to get me to seriously consider investing in a pair for myself, don't you think? He was **creating value in my mind.** He talked about how the shoes were made. He mentioned they were bench-crafted, which meant one person was completely responsible for making this specific pair of shoes.

Feature (which means)	Advantage (which means)	Benefit (to client)
calfskin leather	molds to your foot	custom made feel
full leather lining	finished feel	instant comfort
traditional loafer	will stay in style	wear for years

He then went in for the kill, "Since they are bench-crafted, they have the artisan's name on them. When they're finished, these shoes have no nicks, no scratches, and all the components fit perfectly. Unlike shoes made on an assembly line, these shoes are one of a kind." Now there is a value proposition, if I ever heard one!

Then he asked me a 'simple' closing question, *"What size do you wear?"* He then proceeded to have me slip on a pair in my size.

Long story made short: He was right, they 'are' delightful to wear. When I walked out of his store, both of us had big smiles on our faces. I could hardly wait for the snow to leave back home so I could take them out for a walk here in Northern Alberta. I love them! In fact, I took them to Australia that next January for a walk-about.

Simple story of how one wise young salesman took 'personal leadership' and leveraged his craft to the next level by engaging his client. He told a story that created 'value' in my mind and allowed me to 'see myself' in those shoes.

Do you do that with your customers when they come into your store? Or when you visit them in their place of business?

Client service redefined... as a sales success tool

These are two questions you need to ask yourself and your clients on a frequent basis.

- "How can I reinvent myself, or my company to better serve and provide for your changing needs?"
- "Is there some service or additional product I should be providing to make your experience easier, more rewarding or user friendly?"

Remember, if you aren't asking these questions your competitors are.

Visit **www.SuccessPublications.ca** to get your personal copies of **"Thinking Beyond the FIRST Sale"** and **'Make ME Feel Special'** for your sales success library. You'll be glad you did, and so will your clients and customers.

Copyright and license notes

SELL! Idea-rich techniques for sales success

Bob 'Idea Man' Hooey, Accredited Speaker, 2011 Spirit of CAPS recipient. Prolific author of 30 plus business, leadership, and career success publications

Photos of Bob: **Dov Friedman**, www.photographybyDov.com
Bonnie-Jean McAllister, www.elantraphotography.com
Editorial, layout and design: **Irene Gaudet,** Vitrak Creative Services, www.vitrakcreative.com

ISBN: 9781998014071 IS

Printed in the United States 10 9 8 7 6 5 4 3 2 1
Success Publications – a division of Creativity Corner Inc.
Box 10, Egremont, AB T0A 0Z0
www.successpublications.ca
Creative office: 1-780-736-0009

"You are never too old to set another goal or to dream a new dream." C.S. Lewis

Acknowledgements, credits, and disclaimers

תודה
Dankie **Gracias**
Спасибо **Merci** شکراً **Takk**
Köszönjük Terima kasih
Grazie Dziękujemy Děkojame
Ďakujeme Vielen Dank **Paldies**
Kiitos **Täname teid** 谢谢
Thank You Tak
感謝您 Obrigado Teşekkür Ederiz
Σας Ευχαριστούμ 감사합니다
Bedankt **Děkujeme vám** ขอบคุณ
ありがとうございます
Tack

As with each of my books, a very special dedication of this piece of myself, to the two people who meant the most to me, my folks **Ron and Marge Hooey**. Sadly, both my parents left this earthly realm in 1999. I still miss our time together and your encouragement and love. I was blessed with the two of you in my life. I've added **George and Lillian Sidor** (Irene's folks) to this gratitude list.

To my inspiring wife and professional proofreader and publications coach, **Irene Gaudet**, who loves, encourages, and supports me in my quest to continue sharing my **Ideas At Work!** across the world. Thank you seems so inadequate for your timely work in helping make my writing and my client service better! I love the time we spend together!

To my **colleagues and friends** in Toastmasters, the National Speakers Association (NSA), the Canadian Association of Professional Speakers (CAPS), and the Global Speakers Federation (GSF) who continually challenge me to strive for success and increased excellence.

To my **great audiences, leaders, students, coaching clients, and readers** across the globe who share their experiences and enjoyment of my work. Your positive and supportive feedback encourages me to keep working on additional programs and success publications like this updated version. My experience with you creates the foundation for additional real-life experiences I can take from the stage to the page, the classroom to the boardroom.

My thanks to a select few friends for your ongoing support and 'constructive' abuse. You know who you are. ☺

Disclaimer

We have not attempted to cite all the authorities and sources consulted in the preparation of this book. To do so would require much more space than is available. The list would include departments of various governments, libraries, industrial institutions, periodicals, and many individuals. Inspiration was drawn from many sources, including other books by the author; in this updated creation of this min-version of **'SELL!'**

'Sell!' is written and designed to provide information on more creative use of your time, as a business leader's enhancement guide. It is sold with the 'explicit' understanding that the publisher and/or the author are not engaged in rendering legal, accounting, or other Professional services. If legal or other expert assistance is required, the services of a competent Professional in your geographic area should be sought.

It is not the purpose of this mini book to reprint all the information that is otherwise available. Its primary purpose is to complement, amplify, and supplement other books and reference materials already available. You are encouraged to search out and study all the available material, learn as much as possible, and tailor the information to your individual needs. This will help to enhance your success in being a more effective salesperson, leader or professional.

Every effort has been made to make this book as complete and as accurate as possible within the scope of its focus. However, there may be mistakes, both typographical and in content or attribution. Graphics are royalty free or under license. Care has been taken to trace ownership of copyright material contained in this volume. The publisher will gladly receive information that will allow him to rectify any reference or credit line in subsequent editions. This book should be used only as a general guide and not as the ultimate source of information. Furthermore, this book contains information that is current only up to the date of publication.

The purpose of 'SELL!' is to educate and entertain; perhaps to inform and to inspire. It is certainly to challenge its readers to learn and apply its secrets and tips, to challenge them to enhance their skills and leverage their efforts to create more Productive outcomes. The author and publisher shall have neither liability nor responsibility to any person or entity with respect to any loss or damage caused, or alleged to have been caused, directly or indirectly, by the information contained in this book.

Bob's B.E.S.T. publications

Bob is a *prolific* author who has been capturing and sharing his wisdom and experience in print and electronic formats for the past fifteen plus years. In addition to the following publications, several of them best sellers, he has written for consumer, corporate, trade, professional associations, and on-line publications. He has been engaged to write and assist on publications by other best-selling writers and successful companies.

Bob's **B**usiness **E**nhancement **S**uccess **T**ools

Leadership, business, and career success series:
Running TOO Fast (8th edition 2022)
Legacy of Leadership (6th edition 2024)
Make ME Feel Special! (6th edition 2022)
Why Didn't I 'THINK' of That? (6th edition 2022)
Speaking for Success! (10th edition 2023)
THINK Beyond the First Sale (3rd edition 2022)
Prepare Yourself to WIN! (3rd edition 2018)

Bob's mini-book success series:
The Courage to Lead! (4th edition 2024)
Creative Conflict (3rd edition 2024)
Get to YES! (5th edition 2023)
THINK Before You Ink! (3rd edition 2017)
Running to Win! (2nd edition 2024)
Generate More Sales (5th edition 2023)
Unleash your Business Potential (3rd edition 2023)
Learn to Listen (2nd edition 2017)

Creativity Counts! (3rd edition 2024)
Create Your Future! (3rd edition 2024)

Bob's Pocket Wisdom series: *2023)*
Pocket Wisdom for **Selling Professionals**
Pocket Wisdom for **Speakers** (updated 2023)
Pocket Wisdom for **Innovators**
Pocket Wisdom for **Leaders – Power of One!** (updated 2023)
Pocket Wisdom for **Business Builders**

Bob's Idea-rich leaders edge series: *(new 2018-2024)*
LEAD! 12 idea-rich leadership success strategies
CREATE! Idea-rich strategies for enhanced innovation
TIME! Idea-rich tips for enhanced performance and productivity
SERVE! Idea-rich strategies for enhanced customer service
SPEAK! Idea-rich tips and techniques for great presentations
CREATIVE CONFLICT Idea-rich leadership for team success
SELL! Idea-rich techniques for sales success

Co-authored books created by Bob
Quantum Success – 3 volume series (2006)
In the Company of Leaders (3rd edition 2014)
Foundational Success (2nd edition 2013)

Visit: **www.SuccessPublications.ca** for more information on Bob's publications and other success resources. We can arrange special bulk rates for you and your teams.

Email: **bob@ideaman.net** or visit:
www.SuccessPublications.ca

"We cannot solve our problems with the same thinking we used when we created them."
Albert Einstein

What they say about Bob 'Idea Man' Hooey

I frequently travel across North America, and more recently around the globe, sharing my **Ideas At Work!** I am fortunate to get feedback and comments from my audiences and colleagues. These comments come from people who have been touched, challenged, or simply enjoyed themselves in one of my sessions.

"I still get comments from people about your presentation. Only a few speakers have left an impression that lasts that long. You hit a spot with the tourism people." **Janet Bell**, Yukon Economic Forums

"Thank you, Bob, it is always a pleasure to see a true professional at work. You have made the name 'Speaker' stand out as a truism - someone who encourages people to examine their lives and adjust. The comments indicated you hit people right where it is important - in their hearts. Each of those in your audience took away a new feeling of personal success and encouragement." **Sherry Knight**, Dimension Eleven Human Resources and Communications

*"I am pleased to recommend **Bob 'Idea Man' Hooey** to any organization looking for a charismatic, confident speaker and seminar leader. I have seen Bob in action on several occasions, and he is ALWAYS on! Bob has the ability to grab his audience's attention and keep it. Quite simply, if Bob is involved - your program or seminar is guaranteed to succeed."* **Maurice Laving**, Coordinator Training and Development, London Drugs

*"On very short notice Bob cleared his schedule and graciously presented at our meeting when the original Speaker was unable to attend. **Last week Bob set the tone for our two-day leadership meeting and gave us all a motivational lift.** His compassion and true interest in people was clearly evident, making him very credible. He shared some great stories, has a wealth of experience and knowledge and it was a pleasure listening to him. His down-to-Earth style makes it easier to retain the information presented. He also followed up with additional info and handouts, cementing his message of building bridges, not walls. Fantastic job, Bob, and thanks again!"* **Barbara Afra Beler**, MBA, Senior Specialist Commercial Community, Alberta North, **BMO Bank of Montreal**

*"I have been so excited working with **Bob Hooey**, as he has given inspiration and motivation to our leadership team members. Both at the Brick Warehouse – Alberta and here at Art Van Furniture – Michigan; with his years of experience in working with business executives and his humorous and delightful packaging of his material, he makes **learning with Bob a real joy**. But most importantly, anyone who encounters his material is the better for it."*

Kim Yost, CEO Art Van Furniture, former CEO The Brick

Motivate your teams, your employees, and your leaders to 'productively' grow and 'profitably' succeed!

Protect your conference investment - leverage your training dollars.

Enhance your professional career and sell more products and services.

Equip and motivate your leaders and their teams to grow and succeed, 'even' in tough times!

Leverage your time to enhance your skills, equip your teams, and better serve your clients.

Leverage your leadership and investment of time to leave a significant legacy!

Call today to engage best-selling author, award winning, inspirational leadership keynote speaker, leaders' success coach, and employee development trainer, **Bob 'Idea Man' Hooey** and his innovative, audience based, results-focused, **Ideas At Work!** for your next company, convention, leadership, staff, training, or association event. You'll be glad you did!

Call 1-780-736-0009 to connect with Bob 'Idea Man' Hooey today!

Learn more about Bob at: **www.ideaman.net** or **www.BobHooey.training**